ILLINOIS

A Turner Educational Services, Inc. book. Based on the Portrait
of America television series created by R.E. (Ted) Turner.

Library of Congress Number: 86-17739

1234567890   9089888786

Library of Congress Cataloging in Publication Data

Thompson, Kathleen.
  Illinois.

  (Portrait of America)
  "A Turner book."
  Summary: Discusses the history, economy, culture,
and future of Illinois. Also includes a state
chronology, pertinent statistics, and maps.
    1. Illinois—Juvenile literature. [1. Illinois]
I. Title. II. Series: Thompson, Kathleen. Portrait
of America.
F541.3.T48   1986   977.3   86-17739
ISBN 0-86514-452-4 (lib. bdg.)
ISBN 0-86514-527-X (softcover)

Cover Photo: Illinois Department of Commerce and Community Affairs

★ ★ ★ ★
★ ★
Portrait of AMERICA

ILLINOIS

Kathleen Thompson

A TURNER BOOK
RAINTREE PUBLISHERS

Rockford

Chicago

Marseilles • • Joliet

Illinois River

Peoria
•
Pekin
•
San Jose • Farmer City • • Champaign
Quincy • Athens • • Urbana
⭐ • Decatur
SPRINGFIELD

Mississippi River

• Cahokia

Vienna
•
Cairo

CONTENTS

Introduction

Illinois, the Land of Lincoln, the Prairie State.

"It gives me a lot of pleasure to plow the same fields that my father plowed and my grandfather plowed."

Illinois: politicians, prairies, soybeans, baseball, tractors, theaters.

"We're gonna get this group together, we're gonna loop the loop forever, we're gonna ride and ride and ride. Everybody on!"

Illinois is a midwestern farm state that has within its borders a city which rivals in size and sophistication the huge coastal metropolises. It is a manufacturing state that produces more soybeans than any other state in the nation. The mythology of Illinois includes log splitters and hog butchers, gangsters and corrupt politicians. In spite of its rich history and its bright future, Illinois is a state that remains very much of the present.

Farms provide much of the scenery throughout Illinois, the Prairie State.

The Prairie State

If you want to talk about the history of Illinois, you have to talk about the prairie. Illinois is a large state. It reaches as far north as Portsmith, New Hampshire and as far south as Portsmith, Virginia. And at one time, just about all of that was prairie. It was flat land where the grass grew so tall and so thick that a new kind of plow had to be invented to break it up. The story of Illinois is the story of how people worked with—and against—that prairie.

The earliest people we know of in Illinois were the Indians we call the Mound Builders. We don't know what they called themselves. These prehistoric people built temples and pyramids that were very much like those of the Aztecs and

The prairie grass in Illinois is so tall and thick that a new plow had to be invented.

Mayans in South America. One of their "mounds" that is still standing is as large as the Great Pyramids of Egypt.

When the first Europeans entered what is now Illinois, the various tribes of the area had formed a government, a union called the Illinois Confederacy. They had banded together in much the same way that the original thirteen colonies had— for cooperation and defense. These tribes included the Cahokia, Kaskaskia, Michigamea, Moingwea, Peoria, and Tamaroa. Later, they were attacked by Iroquois Indians who had been pushed into the area by white settlement.

No one knows for certain who the first white people to enter Illinois were. But they were probably Jacques Marquette and Louis Joliet. Marquette and Joliet were exploring the route of the Mississippi River. These two were followed by other French explorers and priests.

As usual, the French did not enter the area to take land away from the Indians. Their interest was in bringing the Roman Catholic church to the Indians

and in trading with them. So, for many years, any fighting that went on was not between whites and Indians. It was between the French and Indians on one side and the British on the other.

In 1699, French priests set up a mission and trading post in Cahokia. It became the first permanent white town in Illinois. Other priests created the town of Kaskaskia in 1703. Cahokia and Kaskaskia, together, were

the heart of French life in the area for a long time.

But there was some disagreement about who owned the region. In 1717, the French declared that it was part of their Louisiana Colony, which stretched along the eastern side of the Mississippi from the Great Lakes to the Gulf

Photos by Illinois Historic Preservation Agency

The earliest Indians in Illinois were known as Mound Builders. Twin Mounds (above) are platform and conical mounds. At the right is Arrowpoint Cache with arrowpoints to honor a buried leader.

of Mexico. The British disagreed. They said that all the land due west of their colonies on the east coast belonged to them.

In 1763, an Indian chief named Pontiac declared war against the British in an attempt to protect the Indian land. The French fought with him. But the British won and the French gave up their claims to the Illinois area.

Back in the thirteen colonies, American settlers were preparing to fight against the British for their independence. The future of the people of Illinois— the Indians and the few thousand white settlers—would be decided in battles at Concord and Lexington, in conference rooms in Philadelphia, and finally in Kaskaskia and Cahokia.

In 1778, a Virginian named George Rogers Clark led a group of frontiersmen-turned-soldiers against the British and captured these two towns. When the Revolutionary War ended, Illinois was part of Virginia.

At that time, many of the thirteen states claimed land in the western part of the country. However, Maryland, a state which did not own western lands, objected to this situation. It was afraid that the western lands would give these states too much power in the new federal government. And so Maryland refused to approve the Articles of Confederation until the other states gave up their claims to areas like Illinois. In 1784, Illinois became federal land belonging to no particular state. A few years later, it was declared part of the Northwest Territory. And in 1800, Congress made Illinois a part of the Indiana Territory.

It was not until 1809 that the Illinois Territory was formed. It included Illinois and Wisconsin.

Now, the fighting in the Illinois Territory was between the Indians and the white settlers. More and more Indian land was taken from them by force. When the United States and Great Britain went to war in 1812, the Indians made a desperate attempt to regain their lands by siding with their old enemy, the British. They fought hard against the Americans, scoring a major victory at Fort Dearborn. But the United States won the war.

In 1818, Illinois became a state.

The Black Hawk War was the last great struggle between Illinois Indians and white settlers.

From the very beginning it was a mixture of different elements—farming and trading, rural and urban. Some of the very first settlers after statehood bought land in places where they expected great cities to grow up. They were called speculators because they bought the land in order to resell it later when it would be more valuable. At the same time, farmers were settling on the rich farmlands in the western part of the state.

When the Erie Canal was finished in 1825, it became a lot easier to travel to Illinois and its neighboring states. The population grew by leaps and bounds. Again, the Indians were pushed out of their homelands. In 1832, the last great struggle between Illinois Indians and white settlers ended in the defeat of the Sauk and Fox Indians in the Black Hawk War. It was during the war that a young man from southern Illinois first tried his hand as a leader of men. Captain Abraham Lincoln and his troops never saw battle, but his feet were set on the path he would follow for the rest of his life.

It's strange to think now that Indians were still struggling to stay on their lands at the same time immigrants were moving into the cities to work in factories. These two parts of our history often seem so separate. The Indian wars belong to the old while factories and labor problems belong to the new. But the old and new, in history, often exist side by side.

In 1839, the state capital was moved from Vandalia to Springfield. Abraham Lincoln's name again enters Illinois' history. He led the delegation in the legislature which succeeded in winning the capital for Sangamon

County.

In the next two decades, transportation to and from the Great Lakes states opened up on all fronts. The Illinois and Michigan Canal was finished. Railroads were built. Farm products from Illinois were now moved easily to markets in the east.

In 1858, Illinois and Abraham

At the left is an example of Great Lakes shipping today. Above, the Illinois and Michigan canal opened transportation to the Great Lakes states.

Lincoln began to be talked about all over the country. Lincoln was running against Stephen Douglas for U.S. Senator. They debated all over the state and one issue stood out in their debates—slavery. Lincoln's stand against slavery and the appeal of his personality were very powerful. He lost the Senate race to Douglas, but only two years later he was elected president of the United States.

Then seven Southern states withdrew from the Union. The Civil War had begun. The country lawyer from Illinois led the United States through the most painful time in its history. In the terrible struggle, he relied on another man from Illinois, General Ulysses S. Grant.

15

The Civil War, fought during Lincoln's presidency, is shown in a reenactment above.

It was during the Civil War, at a service for soldiers who had died in battle, that Lincoln made his most famous speech, the Gettysburg Address. And the words "of the people, by the people, and for the people" became part of our political heritage.

Not only Grant and Lincoln, but all of the people of Illinois were greatly affected by the war. More than a quarter of a million men went to fight in the Union army.

After the Civil War ended, Abraham Lincoln was killed in the Ford Theater in Washington by actor John Wilkes Booth, a Confederate sympathizer.

In the years to come, industry grew rapidly in Illinois. More and more immigrants came to find work in its mills and factories. Chicago, with its very favorable location on Lake Michigan, became a great industrial center. In 1871, a large part of the city was destroyed in the Chicago Fire, but it was soon rebuilt.

But industrialization brought problems to Illinois. The working conditions in the factories were almost unbearable. The hours were long, the work backbreaking, and conditions unsafe and unhealthy. Many of the European immigrants came from a tradition of political action and protest. They refused to accept their lot.

At a meeting in Haymarket Square in Chicago, police were sent in to break things up. A bomb was thrown into the police line. Rioting broke out. Ten people were killed. Eight anarchists were arrested and convicted of throwing the bomb that started the riot. Even the next governor of Illinois, John P. Altgeld, declared that the trial was unfair, but that did not stop the hangings.

Altgeld's election in 1892 brought changes to Illinois. He tackled the labor problems head-on and was able to make some improvements in working conditions, the public school system, and prisons. These reforms continued even after Altgeld left office. Child labor laws were

The symbol of Chicago's incredible tragedy, the Great Fire, is the water tower located a mile north of the river. Below is a photo taken in 1871, a day after the fire burned itself out.

passed. Illinois became the first state to pass a law instituting aid to dependent children.

And then Prohibition became the law of the land. Once it was no longer legal to sell alcoholic beverages, a tremendous business in illegal liquor boomed. Chicago was right in the middle of it all. Gangsters like Al Capone became the world's image of this great city. Gang warfare broke out in the streets. Corrupt politicians worked hand in hand with bootlegging mobs. All of that remains part of the mythology of Illinois' largest city.

All the time, industry kept growing. But farmers suffered in the 1920s when farm prices dropped. Everyone suffered in the 1930s when the Great Depression hit. Factories closed. People were out of work. And yet, in 1933, Chicago hosted the great

World's Fair—The Century of Progress Exposition.

Another element was added to the image of Illinois in 1942 when scientists at the University of Chicago set off the first controlled nuclear reaction. The atomic age had begun—in Illinois.

In the last several decades, Illinois has continued to grow industrially. The cities have become larger and larger, especially Chicago. This has created problems between rural and urban areas in their struggles for political power and pieces of the state's financial pie. The cities have also faced the serious racial and other social problems that all large cities in this country face. Chicago has been called by some the most segregated large city in the United States.

In 1968, Illinois was in the national news when the Democratic Convention met at the Hilton Hotel. Outside, demonstrators gathered in a city park to protest United States involvement in Viet Nam. When police were brought in to clear the park, Chicago was once again the scene of riots that would be of political significance around the world.

Today, Illinois remains a rich and sometimes troubled mixture of much that is good and bad in our country. Home of our largest midwestern city, it is also a thriving agricultural state. The scene of some great injustices, it is also the birthplace of some of our most progressive ideas.

It is the state that produced Abraham Lincoln and Al Capone. And that just about sums it up.

Illinois Department of Commerce and Community Affairs

On the left-hand page is Al Capone, a famous Chicago gangster. At the left is a panorama of the Chicago skyline.

The People vs. the Prairie

"The grass was a much tougher enemy than the forest."

When the first settlers moved west from the woodlands of the eastern United States, they found a kind of land—and a kind of problem—they'd never known before. To clear Massachusetts and Pennyslvania and New Hampshire for farming, trees had to be cut and stones gathered. But in Illinois, there was prairie.

The prairie soil was rich and thick. The roots of prairie grass were thick and tangled. One person, one family, working alone couldn't clear and plow the prairie land.

In 1846, Ron Nelson's ancestors came to Illinois and started a community called Bishop Hill. The people worked together, sharing the labor, the property, and the profits.

At the right is a self portrait of painter Olof Krans.
On the left-hand page is one of his paintings showing
immigrants at work. Below is the Bishop Hill Colony
Store.

Illinois Historical Preservation Agency

Bishop Hill Heritage Association

Today, Ron Nelson is rebuilding the town of Bishop Hill. For him, it's a labor of love.

"Well, I think this is my identity. I have worked on so much in Bishop Hill now—actually done physical work, actually planned the work—that I feel like, you know, I have a stake in it, almost as much as those people who put *it up. . . . I think it's good to be able to feel that way about something."*

Ron Nelson has had help in rebuilding Bishop Hill, help from a man who died years ago. Olof Krans was a housepainter when he started out in the Bishop Hill colony. And when he was an old man, he painted pic-

Photos by Bishop Hill Heritage Association

tures of the people, the buildings, and the life he remembered from his childhood. Because of him, we have a record of how these early Swedish immigrants conquered the prairie.

And Ron Nelson has a blueprint for his restoration of Bishop Hill.

Ron Nelson (below left-hand page) and crew are rebuilding Bishop Hill. At the left is the Krusbo House at Bishop Hill built in 1855. Above is the grain elevator built in 1870 at Bishop Hill.

Abraham Lincoln was born in Tennessee and went on to belong to the nation and the world. But nobody can deny that Illinois has

Let the Band Play Dixie

"He said we are gathered not in anger, but in celebration. Let's be grateful we are once again a single nation."
Bob Gibson stands on a stage in Chicago singing his song about the wisdom and compassion of Abraham Lincoln. Half a state away in Petersburg, Harlington Wood looks back on a family history that is filled with the romance of Lincoln's legend.

"You know, around this town you can't hardly help it. You kind of grow up in the atmosphere. . . . and I didn't resist it. I just loved the story, and being a lawyer, it had a particular interest to me."

Above is the Lincoln home at Springfield. At the right is President Lincoln's bedroom. In the foreground is Abraham Lincoln.

a special claim. He grew to manhood in New Salem. He practiced law in Springfield. He went to the White House from Illinois.

And the things that Abraham Lincoln stood for—equality and respect for others—have a special meaning here. There is a special pain when those values fail as they did on Palm Sunday in 1983.

A black candidate for mayor entered a church in a white neighborhood. What happened then came very near to being a riot. The church's priest, Father Francis Ciezadlo, remembers.

"It broke my heart. That's all. No, it broke my heart. Here I am, all these years as a priest teaching one thing, Christian love. . . . in one of the biggest Catholic cities in the world. Teaching Christian love—and what do we do? Right here in my own community where I thought we had people who could understand, people who could love. . . ."

It was a sad moment. But

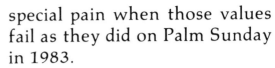

Father Francis Ciezadlo brought black and white worshipers together. Above is St. Pascal's Church.

With respect and understanding, blacks and whites of St. Pascal's and St. Clara's work together.

Father Ciezadlo had an idea. He and his church members found a black parish that was willing to join them from time to time in worship. And the people of St. Pascal's parish soon discovered that the people of St. Clara's parish were very much like them.

It was just as Abraham Lincoln always believed it could be. Wounds can be healed. People can come together. All it takes is respect and understanding.

"'Let's stand together reassured now that peace has been secured. Our nation's illness can be cured, and I can suggest the overture for this occasion.' He said, 'let the band play Dixie, play that tune that holds its head up high and proud, and let our nation once divided, bloody but unbowed, take swords of war and beat them back into a plow.' On the day that Lee surrendered, Mr. Lincoln told the crowd, let the band play Dixie."*

Corn, Combines, Coal, and Just About Everything Else

Illinois is a leading manufacturing state. It's a leading agricultural state. It's a leading mining state. It's even a leading tourist state. There's a lot happening in Illinois.

Because of its location—in the middle of the country and bordering on both Lake Michigan and the Mississippi River—Illinois became involved in manufacturing almost from the beginning. But it is a lot larger than most of the heavily industrial eastern states. There has always been plenty of room for farming. In fact, less than a century ago, most of Illinois' workers were employed in agriculture.

Today, however, well over a fifth of the people employed in Illinois are in manufacturing. Even more work in whole-

A candy manufacturer at Goelitz Confectionery Company.

29

sale and retail selling, and almost that many are involved in service occupations. Only about 3 percent work on farms.

However, a lot of Illinois manufacturing is related to agriculture. A little over 80 percent of the value of goods produced in the state comes from manufacturing. Just under 20 percent of that total comes from the production of nonelectric machinery, which includes farm machinery as well as machinery for construction and metalworking.

Illinois is one of the nation's largest producers of farm machinery. It was in Illinois that John Deere invented the plow that made it possible to farm the prairie. The present headquarters of John Deere, Moline, is known as the Farm Implement Capital of the World.

The second largest area of manufacturing in Illinois is also farm-related. A little over ten percent of the state's manufacturing income comes from food processing. Corn is the chief

On the left-hand page is a John Deere tractor. John Deere workers are shown above (top). Immediately above is John Deere, inventor of the plow.

agricultural crop in the state and Illinois is also the leader in making corn products. It's number one in candy manufacturing and right up there in butter and cheese.

After food processing comes the manufacture of electric machinery and equipment. The Chicago area is the most important manufacturing center in the United States for products such as telephone equipment and radios and televisions.

These are only a few of the hundreds of different kinds of products made in Illinois. Altogether, they range from sporting goods to drugs to steel. At the same time, Illinois remains a leading agricultural state.

Corn is the state's biggest crop. Almost 20 percent of the corn grown in this country comes from Illinois. But Illinois also grows more soybeans than any other state, as well as oats, wheat, and other grain crops.

Illinois farmers raise hogs, lots of hogs. But then, they raise almost everything—beef cattle, sheep, lambs, poultry. And in the northern part of the state, vegetables are grown.

With all that manufacturing and agricultural activity, it doesn't seem that there would be room for anything else. But there is. Illinois is one of the nation's leading coal producers.

In addition, Illinois produces oil and several other important minerals.

Then there are the tourists. Compared to the money brought in by manufacturing ($45 billion) and the money brought in by farming ($7 billion), tourism's $3.75 billion may seem like small potatoes. But it is a total that many other states would envy.

Photos by Illinois Department of Commerce and Community Affairs

Illinois is home for the Chicago Cubs. On the left-hand page are team members in action and a fan. Above left is Stanley Field Hall at the Field Museum of Natural History in Chicago. Above right is a picturesque church in Galena. Garden of Gods State Park is below.

The tourists come to see where Abraham Lincoln lived and worked. They come to see the beautifully restored town of Galena, where Ulysses S. Grant lived. They visit the fifty state parks. And most of all, they come to Chicago—for the museums, the theaters, the restaurants, the ethnic neighborhoods.

All in all, if you can't find it in Illinois, you're going to have trouble finding it anywhere.

33

THE JESSE WHITE TUMBLING TEAM   Coke

Tumbling Out of Cabrini Green

"I was raised up in that area and I could have very easily gone down the wrong road. But someone took me under their arm and they taught me the right way."

The area Jesse White grew up in is Cabrini Green, one of Chicago's huge housing projects. The projects came out of a dream that someone once had to tear down the decaying buildings of the slums and put up clean new apartments for lower income families. That dream failed. Without jobs, educational opportunities, and full participation in society, the people in the projects remained locked in to poverty.

Soon, Cabrini Green was a place to escape from. For some, the escape routes have been destructive—drugs, gangs, crime. For Jesse White, it was different.

"I got involved in basketball, base-ball, track, and field. I have never for-gotten what was done for me, and I think that that is one of the things that has spurred me on."

Today, Jesse White is a public school gym teacher in the Cabrini Green area. He's offering his students the kind of escape route that worked for him. He's turning them into tumblers.

Somersaults, back flips, cart-wheels—the Jesse White tumblers seem to fly through the air. They actually fly around the world—with the aid of airplanes —performing and displaying their marvelous skills. But there's more to being part of the team than a good handstand.

"The rules are simple. You cannot smoke, drink, get into trouble with the law, or be gang-related. You follow those guidelines and you can be a member —as well as be a good performer and a gentleman."

In the end, the escape route from Cabrini Green is the road to self-respect.

On the left-hand page is the exciting Jesse White Tumbling Team. The tumblers are shown in some thrilling stunts at left.

Chicago and Beyond

There's almost too much to say about cultural life in Illinois. It's so rich, so varied that the temptation is just to start listing. There are the writers, for example. Among the important writers who have lived and worked in Illinois are people like Edgar Lee Masters, Vachel Lindsay, Carl Sandburg, Gwendolyn Brooks, John Dos Passos, Theodore Dreiser, Saul Bellow, Nelson Algren, James T. Farrell, Archibald MacLeish, David Mamet. . . . The list goes on and on.

And there are the architects. The city of Chicago has long been the center of modern architecture with buildings designed by Frank Lloyd Wright, Louis Sullivan, Ludwig Mies van der Rohe.

In music there is the world famous Chicago Symphony.

A sculpture by the Spanish artist Joan Miro is adjacent to 69 West Washington Street in Chicago.

And there is the history of great jazz, blues, folk, and gospel music.

After a while listing just doesn't seem good enough. There's something about the art of Illinois that makes it worth looking at more closely.

Take, for example, Edgar Lee Masters' *Spoon River Anthology*. This group of poems looks with love and irony at the lives of ordinary people. Behind it, there are strong midwestern values and an unusual kind of sophistication. That blend can be seen in much of the cultural life of Illinois.

In the last few years, Chicago theaters have won worldwide

Poet Edgar Lee Masters is at the left. Below are members of Chicago's well-known comedy troupe, Second City.

Rob Potter

The Chicago Symphony Orchestra is one of the world's most respected orchestras.

fame. Today, Chicago has well over one hundred active theaters. But it's not Broadway or anything like it. The most respected of Chicago's theaters started in storefronts with small budgets and more courage than common sense. Some of the companies whose work is known around the world still perform in spaces that have fewer than two hundred seats.

Second City, an improvisational comedy theater, has sent out into the world actors like Mike Nichols and Elaine May, Alan Arkin, Valerie Harper, Barbara Harris, and John Belushi —to name only a few. And the performances at Second City are still done with a few chairs, a few props, and not much in the way of costumes.

You can go outside of Chicago to the smaller cities. Many, like Peoria, have a symphony orchestra, a ballet troupe, theater group, and art centers.

Art and culture in Illinois reach out to the world. But they are firmly grounded in the hard-working lives of the people, in the neighborhoods, the towns, the prairie of the Midwest.

A Man of Parts

"She's about as good at baking pies as you are at painting."

John Vaughn, southern Illinois farmer, is sitting at his kitchen table with Shozo Sato, world famous artist and theater director. They are about to dig into one of Lucille Vaughn's pumpkin pies. These three friends have one important thing in common. All of them do what they do very well.

What John does these days is not only farming. Like many others across the country, he has another job to help support his family and his farm. John Vaughn is the janitor at the Krannert Center for the Performing Arts at the University of Illinois at Champaign/Urbana. But that hardly describes what John does.

"He is, in one word, marvelous. . . . And whatever he does is just perfect. I've known him for—what?—fifteen years with total respect and trust."

Shozo's words describing John Vaughn are words of high praise. But you hear things like that a lot when you ask people on the

campus about the janitor at the Krannert. Obviously, they're not just talking about his cleaning skill. John has transferred the values and habits of his life in a farm community to his life at the university.

Rural values include helping each other, being there when someone in the community needs

At the right is a scene from a Kabuki play directed by Shozo Sato. John Vaughn is pictured on the right-hand page.

40

you. And John Vaughn has been there for fifteen classes of performing arts students. They have benefited from his knowledge of life as well as from his farm produce.

This isn't the life John Vaughn would have chosen.

"Now of the two, if you were to ask me which I liked best, I would have to be honest and say I liked farming the best because of the outdoor life all the time and seeing the crops grow and gathering in the harvest."

But there's more than one kind of harvest. And John Vaughn has a talent for making things grow—soybeans and music students alike.

A Future Tied to the Present

A look at the future of Illinois does not inspire wild guesses about what might happen. Illinois is already very much grown up. It will change in the years to come, there is no doubt of that. But, in a very important way, Illinois already is what it will become.

Economically, Illinois is very strong. Economic activities are varied. Agriculture may decline as it is declining all over the country. But as long as people eat food grown in the soil there are likely to be farms in Illinois. Industry may, and almost certainly will, grow. But the new industries will probably grow from the potential of present industry.

The problems that Illinois faces are similar to the problems faced by other states—crime and poverty in the cities, racial

A winter view of the Wrigley Building, Tribune Tower, and North Michigan Avenue.

The quaint Pomona General Store in southern Illinois.

tensions, and the destruction of natural resources. The real questions about Illinois' future are probably questions about how these common problems will be dealt with.

One indication might be the new state constitution that was approved in 1970. It is a progressive constitution, adopted after a lot of discussion and controversy. Other hopeful signs turn up in the area of race relations. There have been serious problems. Yet, Illinois was the first state to have a black legislator as a leader of one of the houses. And Chicago, only a few years ago, elected its first black mayor.

For a long time, Chicago was called "the city that works." People who lived in the housing projects might have argued with that definition. Still, it said something about, not only Chicago, but all of Illinois.

The people here are independent with a strong streak of common sense. They're practical people. They want things to work. That means though they may sometimes be conservative, they are not too set in their ways to change when it makes sense.

With that attitude, problems can be solved. Illinois can keep moving steadily into a strong future.

Important Historical Events in Illinois

1673 The First Europeans we know of—Louis Joliet and Jacques Marquette—enter Illinois.

1699 The oldest European town in Illinois is founded by French priests as a mission.

1717 Illinois is declared part of Louisiana, the large parcel of land claimed by the French.

1763 Great Britain, having won the French and Indian War, gains control of much French land including Illinois.

1778 The area which includes Illinois becomes part of Virginia.

1784 The federal government takes over control of the Illinois area.

1800 Illinois becomes part of the Indiana Territory.

1809 The Illinois Territory is formed.

1812 Indians in Illinois side with the British in the War of 1812.

1818 Illinois becomes a state.

1832 Defeat of the Sauk and Fox Indians in the Black Hawk War ends Indian resistance to white settlement.

1848 Completion of the Illinois and Michigan Canal opens eastern markets to Illinois farmers.

1858 Abraham Lincoln runs for United States senator against Stephen A. Douglas and gains national recognition.

1871 The Chicago Fire wipes out a large part of the city.

1886 The Haymarket Riot in Chicago, resulting from shocking working conditions, leads to ten deaths.

1893 The World's Columbian Exposition takes place in Chicago.

1900 The flow of the Chicago River is reversed by the Chicago Sanitary and Ship Canal.

1933 The Century of Progress Exposition opens in Chicago.

1942 Enrico Fermi and other scientists at the University of Chicago create the first controlled atomic reaction.

1965 The state senate and legislature are reapportioned.

1968 The Democratic National Convention in Chicago is marked by anti-war riots.

1970 A new state constitution is approved.

Illinois Almanac

Nickname. The Prairie State.

Capital. Springfield.

State Bird. Cardinal.

State Flower. Native violet.

State Tree. White oak.

State Motto. State Sovereignty, National Union.

State Song. Illinois.

State Abbreviations. Ill. (traditional); IL (postal).

Statehood. December 3, 1818, the 21st state.

Government. Congress: U.S. senators, 2; U.S. representatives, 22. **State Legislature:** senators, 59; representatives, 118. **Counties:** 102.

Area. 56,400 sq. mi. (146,075 sq. km.), 24th in size among the states.

Greatest Distances. north/south, 381 mi. (613 km.); east/west, 211 mi. (340 km.). **Shoreline:** 63 mi. (101 km.), along Lake Michigan.

Elevation. Highest: Charles Mound, 1,235 ft. (376 m). **Lowest:** 279 ft. (85 m).

Population. 1980 Census: 11,418,461 (2.7% increase over 1970), 5th among the states. **Density:** 202 persons per sq. mi. (78 persons per sq. km.). **Distribution:** 83% urban, 17% rural. **1970 Census:** 11,110,285.

Economy. Agriculture: corn, soybeans, wheat, oats, hay, cattle, hogs, poultry. **Manufacturing:** machinery, primary and fabricated metals, electric and electronic equipment, food products, chemical products, printed materials, instruments. **Mining:** coal, petroleum, stone, sand and gravel.

Places to Visit

Abraham Lincoln's Home in Springfield.

Black Hawk Statue, near Oregon.

Brookfield Zoo in Chicago.

Chicago.

Dickson Mounds, near Lewistown.

Morton Arboretum, near Lisle.

Ulysses S. Grant Home in Galena.

Annual Events

Boat and Sports Show at McCormick Place in Chicago (January).

Flower and Garden Show in Chicago (March).

Old Town Art Fair in Chicago (June).

Mississippi Music Festival in Edwardsville (mid-July through August).

Illinois State Fair in Springfield (August).

Du Quoin State Fair in Du Quoin (September).

Illinois Counties

INDEX